Crafts for Fun

Using Recycled and Everyday Items

Virginia S. Rich

Illustrated by
Sandy Clay Bauer

Judson Press® Valley Forge

This book is a celebration for Dave

The articles in this book were first published in the following issues of *Youth Magazine:* April, June, July, August, September, October, December 1977; February, March, May, July, September, October 1978; January, February, June, September, November 1979; December 1979–January 1980; June 1980; January 1981.
Copyright © United Church Press.

Library of Congress Cataloging-in-Publication Data
Rich, Virginia S.
    Crafts for fun.

    Summary: Provides instructions for using recycled or readily available material to make crafts, including baskets, pillows, and window art.
    1. Handicraft—Juvenile literature.   2. Recycling (Waste, etc.)—Juvenile literature.
[1. Handicraft.   2. Recycling (Waste)]   I. Bauer, Sandy, ill.   II. Title.
TT160.R54 1986   745.5   85–18127
ISBN 0–8170–1090–4

The name JUDSON PRESS is registered as a trademark in the U.S. Patent Office.
Printed in the U.S.A.

Contents

Dear Friends,

I really enjoy making things with my hands. As a child, I remember spending time with my aunt as she made pots out of clay. I didn't become a potter but the excitement of learning with my hands has continued.

I have been able to share that kind of excitement with many others. A preschooler learned to make a painting with a marble; a teenager made a belt woven on a bunch of drinking straws; and a grandmother at a church retreat remembered knitting on a spool when she was much younger.

By using this collection of ideas for making and doing these crafts it is hoped that **YOU** as a parent, teacher teenager, or child will also feel the excitement of involving your hands, mind and imagination to create something new.

The three important ingredients needed to do the crafts included in this book are You, the Idea or Instructions, and the Materials.

You, working by yourself or with a group of friends, supply something unique that can bring these projects to life. You may start out by feeling that you are no artist, you're all thumbs. Give yourself a chance. A person who will come to the activity with an experimental frame of mind will probably come up with something different, something funny, and a new way to do things.

The Instructions for each craft give a list of materials needed and the basic steps you will use to get started. Further suggestions about how you may go on with the process, adding your own originality, will often be included. Each craft will be simple enough to allow you to get going easily but it will also give you an opportunity to use your own creativity.

The Materials you work with are very important. With a view to the future and the ever-growing problems of dwindling raw materials, dwindling space for trash disposal, and inflation, the materials to be used in these projects will be either recyclable or readily available, inexpensive ingredients.

Someone has said that the gold mines of the future are the dumps of today. It is hoped that you will find your recyclable materials **before** they reach the dump. For instance those nifty cardboard display cases that are found on the aisles of supermarkets will make fine storage units in your workroom. Have you ever asked the store manager what happens to these displays when they have outlived their purpose? Working on these projects may help you to develop an eye for what *is*

or *is not* usable in the trash bins. The prime attraction of recyclable materials is that they are often free or cost very little.
The advantage of readily available and inexpensive materials is obvious. They are at hand and they won't put a dent in your pocketbook.

So... have fun with these crafts, learn with them, invent with them, play with them. Use this time to get your hands and mind active and involved with these crafts.

Ginny Rich

PAPER BEADS

you need { PAPER, A LARGE NAIL or KNITTING NEEDLE, GLUE, VARNISH, STRING, SCISSORS.

- Cut the paper into long, thin triangles.

(If you can use a paper cutter it will save time and prevent boredom).

- Roll the paper strips around the nail. Start with the wide end of triangle against the nail and roll towards the point.

glue

- Put a dab of glue on the point of the triangle and press it down for a few seconds. When it stays put, slide the bead off the nail. Coat the bead with a light layer of shellac, varnish, glue or clear nail polish.

OKAY, NOW TO IMPROVISE:

- What happens if you use a different material? Try using cloth. Try plastic bread wrappers.

- What happens if you cut straight strips rather than triangles?

- What kind of paper did you use? Did you try magazine covers? Lots of color there! Did you think of brown paper bags? Sunday comics? Wallpaper samples?

Now you have lots of BEADS...

What'll you use them for?
··· besides enough necklaces for you and all your friends

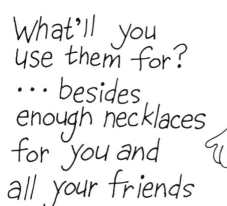

• How about a bead curtain for your window? If you're ambitious, a room divider

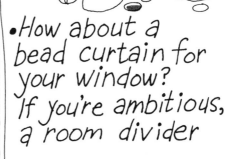

• A Lampshade? Put beads on an old wire lampshade frame

- Did you discover how to vary the size of the beads?

SKINNY triangle + THIN paper =
·Little bead· 🔸

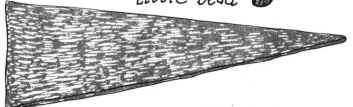

FAT triangle + THICK paper =
·LARGE BEAD· 🔹

- Did you try stringing beads on elastic thread to make a choker?

- Did you try tying loops in your string of beads? ▫

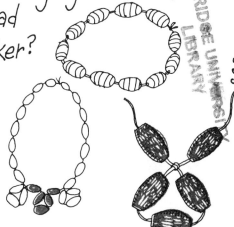

MAKING RECYCLED PAPER

you need

- OLD NEWSPAPERS
- TWO WOODEN FRAMES ~ about 5"x7" ~ purchased or handmade
- WINDOW SCREENING to fit one frame
- STAPLER
- DISH PAN (larger than the wooden frames)
- ELECTRIC BLENDER
- WATER
- SPONGE
- ELECTRIC IRON

Either buy two inexpensive 5" x 7" wooden picture frames at the dime store oR nail together eight pieces of wood to make two 5" x 7" rectangles.

Staple the window screening to the back (FLAT) side of the purchased frame oR to either side of the hand-made one. Leave the second frame open.

Tear up a single page of newspaper and put it in the blender.
Fill the blender with water.
Blend for a minute or two.
The resulting grey liquid is called Slurry. Pour the slurry into the dishpan. Add enough water to raise the liquid in the pan. Make a thick pad of newspapers on your worktable. Have the iron ready to use.

Take apart a newspaper and fold the pages into quarters to be used as blotters. Hold the two frames together like this

PLAIN FRAME
FRAME + SCREENING

The open frame sits on top of the screening. Dip the frames into the slurry. Submerge both of them, then bring them STRAIGHT up out of the water.

blotter

FRAME + SCREEN + SLURRY

Set BOTH frames down on the pad of papers. Remove the TOP frame and put a newspaper "blotter" on top of the slurry. Flip the frame and "blotter" over onto a dry space on the newspaper. Sponge up any excess water through the screen. Remove the screen and place a dry newspaper over the wet rectangle of slurry.

Iron over the paper until it's dry. Carefully lift your new piece of paper from the newspaper pad.

As you make more pieces of paper the layer of slurry which collects on the screen will get thinner and thinner. Now you can mix up more slurry and add it to the mixture in the dishpan. Try some different ingredients such as a paper towel, a piece of tissue or a piece of brown bag.

You can also add finely chopped onion skins, dry leaves or flowers, lint from the clothes dryer, dandelion seeds or whatever you can think of to use as an experiment in texture. □

A FRAME LOOM

You need

- THE WOODEN BOTTOM OF A LARGE APPLIANCE BOX (ask an Appliance Store for discards)
- SANDPAPER • HAMMER • HANDSAW
- 1" NAILS or BRADS • A YARN NEEDLE
- ½" DOWEL ~ at least 18" long
- BALL OF STRING ~ that won't stretch
- YARN to weave with • A TABLE FORK

The bottom of the appliance box should look something like this. Knock the pieces apart with the hammer and choose four good pieces to use. This wood will probably be splintery so SAND all the pieces before working with them.

20" x 24" is the size of this loom but yours could be a different size. Cut two pieces 20" long and two pieces 24" long. Nail them into a rectangle with four nails in each corner for stability.

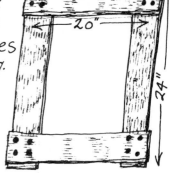

20"

24"

On the bottom 20° crosspiece make a row of nails by partially driving them into the wood at 1/2" intervals. ▼▼▼ Cut the dowel so that it is 18" long. Cut three pieces of string each 12" to 15" long. Lean your frame against a wall or chair with the row of nails at the bottom. Tie the strings loosely around the top cross piece. Put the dowel through the loops. Re-tie the strings so they are all equal. Move the knots to the top of the cross-piece. Now you are ready to put the WARP on the loom. The WARP is the set of strings which run vertically on this loom. Tie one end of the ball of string to one end of the dowel. Bring the string down and around the first nail and then up over the dowel. Continue until you have put WARP around each nail. Make sure the WARP is <u>very</u> tight by pulling up all the slack, then end the WARPING by tying the string tightly around the dowel. The WARP must <u>always</u> be strung tightly. If the WARP loosens, retie the loops holding the dowel.

dowel

nails 1/2" apart

the WARP

Your Loom is now ready for weaving!

The easiest way to weave is the simple over-and-under method.
Be careful not to pull your Yarn too tight while weaving back and forth, or the sides will pull in.

Another way to weave is the Tapestry Weave in which the yarn is wrapped once around each WARP thread:

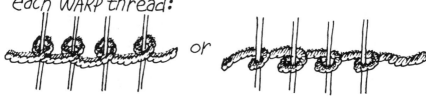

or

When using the over-and-under or tapestry weaves work from the <u>bottom</u> of your loom—next to the nails. After each row of weaving push the yarn down tightly to the previous row. A table fork or a comb are useful tools for doing this job which is called BEATING.

You can make designs by turning your yarn and heading back in the opposite direction <u>before</u> you come to the end of a row.

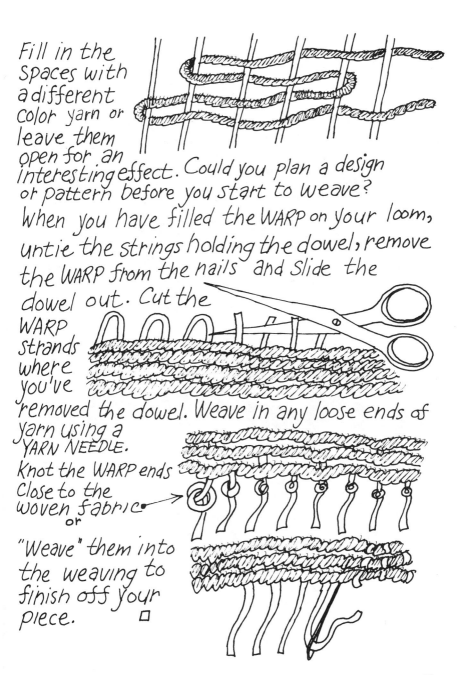

Fill in the spaces with a different color yarn or leave them open for an interesting effect. Could you plan a design or pattern before you start to weave?

When you have filled the WARP on your loom, untie the strings holding the dowel, remove the WARP from the nails and slide the dowel out. Cut the WARP strands where you've removed the dowel. Weave in any loose ends of yarn using a YARN NEEDLE.

Knot the WARP ends close to the woven fabric.

or

"Weave" them into the weaving to finish off your piece. ▫

WEAVING

on a drinking-straw loom

you need
- 4 OR 5 PLASTIC DRINKING STRAWS
- A BALL OF NON-STRETCHING STRING
- MASKING TAPE
- YARN • A YARN NEEDLE

A belt is a good beginning project with a drinking-straw loom. Start with 4 OR 5 straws. Cut one piece of string for each straw. Each string should be twice as long as your waist measurement.

Thread one string
through each straw and fasten it to
the end of the straw with masking tape.
When all the straws are threaded
tie the free ends of the string
together in a loose knot.
Tie your yarn to one of the
straws.
Gather all the
straws in one hand,
keeping the one with
the yarn tied to it on
the outside edge. Weave
the yarn over and under the
straws. Push the
weaving down the
straws as the
top space gets
woven full.
Eventually the woven yarn
will drop off the ends of the
straws onto the strings.
Keep weaving until you have a
piece long enough for a belt.

Remove the straws. Knot the ends neatly—or with a yarn needle weave the ends into the woven part of the belt to make a flat finished end. Redo the knot at the other end or weave the string ends into the piece with a needle.

After you finish weaving your belt there are other things you can weave with your drinking straw loom. A shorter version of the belt can be hung on the wall and used as a holder for pierced earrings.

You can make a purse with four or five long strips. Sew the strips together side by side

Fold this piece in half and stitch up the sides. Add a long or short braided handle.

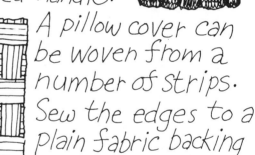

A pillow cover can be woven from a number of strips. Sew the edges to a plain fabric backing to keep the strips in place.

You can experiment with using more than 4 or 5 straws. Devise a way to work on 10 or 12 straws. See how many different ways you can use the woven strips. ☐

23

WINDOW ART

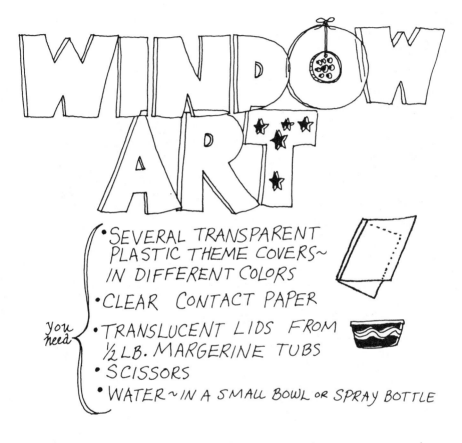

you need
- SEVERAL TRANSPARENT PLASTIC THEME COVERS~ IN DIFFERENT COLORS
- CLEAR CONTACT PAPER
- TRANSLUCENT LIDS FROM ½ LB. MARGERINE TUBS
- SCISSORS
- WATER~ IN A SMALL BOWL OR SPRAY BOTTLE

Bright pieces of transparent plastic can be used in several ways to decorate windows where light can catch their colors.

The simplest way uses the plastic directly on the glass. Cut the plastic into shapes. Dip these into water or spray the window pane ~lightly~ with water. Press the pieces onto the glass. The plastic will stick even after the water has dried When the decoration needs to be removed, there is no sticky adhesive to be cleaned up.

To make a more permanent reusable decoration, bring the clear contact paper into the act.
Cut two circles or squares of the same size out of the contact paper. Trim away a quarter of an inch from the edge of one of the pieces.

¼"

Pull the backing paper off the trimmed piece. With the sticky side up, arrange a design of colored plastic pieces on the trimmed contact paper.

Remove the backing on the larger piece of contact paper and, sticky sides together, carefully press this down over the design you've made. There should be a quarter of an inch extending all around the smaller circle or square. Use this sticky margin to hold the design to the window. To reuse this decoration, store it on a piece of waxed paper.

To make a light-catching medallion that doesn't stick to the glass at all, use a translucent lid from a ½ LB. margerine tub as a base for your design.

Cut a circle of clear Contact paper that will fit _inside_ the ridge on the edge of the lid. Peel the backing off and assemble a design on the sticky side of the Contact paper. Press the paper onto the lid. With your fingernails, smooth the contact paper down tight. This medallion can be hung in a window with a thread loop strung through its edge.

Cut designs by folding the plastic one or two times, Snowflake-style.

Try a mosaic effect by cutting little squares and triangles and combining them into a pattern.□

RUBBER STAMPS

RUBBER STAMPS

You need
- AN OLD INNER TUBE (ask at a garage or gas station)
- RUBBER BANDS
- WOOD SCRAPS • WHITE GLUE
- SCISSORS • CHALK
- STAMP PAD **OR** PAPER TOWEL and STYROFOAM MEAT TRAY
- POSTER PAINT

First, on paper, design your rubber stamp.

Make it simple, with few small details.

cut a square of inner
tube a little
larger than
your design.
The rubber will
be gray and powdery on one
side, black and smooth on the
other. Work on the black side.
Draw your design on the rubber
with chalk. Then cut it out.
At this point you can decide to
add straight lines or smaller
pieces to the design. An easy way
to do this is to use pieces cut
from a rubber band.
Spread a thin layer of glue on the
gray side of the pieces of rubber
you have just cut.

Glue the design firmly to a piece
of flat wood. (If you don't have
any scraps around home,
ask at a lumber yard for
some. They may give you
a few pieces, or sell you
some for very little money.)
Allow the glue to dry for an
hour or so. Then use your rubber
stamp with a ready-made stamp
pad or make one yourself.

To make your own pad, start
with a styrofoam meat tray.
Fold a paper towel to fit
into the tray.
Pour in just enough
poster paint to
moisten it evenly.
Make a few test
prints to get it
just right.

With your rubber stamp you could decorate writing paper. You could design your own trademark or logo to identify your books or notebooks. (Remember that any letters must be <u>backwards</u> on the stamp in order to print <u>frontwards</u>.) Repeat your design on plain paper to make wrapping paper.
You take it from here. □

PILLOWS

FROM RIGHT OFF YOUR BACK

you need {

- OLD T-SHIRTS
  or
- FADED, WORN-OUT JEANS
  or
- THRIFT SHOP BARGAIN CLOTHES

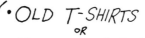

- OLD NYLON STOCKINGS
  or
- SHREDDED FOAM
  or
- DACRON PILLOW STUFFING

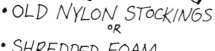

- A NEEDLE and THREAD
  or
- SEWING MACHINE

Look through your clothes. Are there among the things you are outgrowing some you don't want to part with because of sentimental reasons?

The old T-shirt from last year's ball team? The well-worn school shirt? That souvenir of the Bicentennial?

Your patched and embroidered blue jeans? Why not make these old favorites into new pillows for your room?

The basic idea is to sew up all the openings — sleeves, neck, legs, any buttoned openings. Just leave one small opening. Put your stuffing material in through this opening. Then sew it shut too. - - - - - - - -

Two easy stitches to use (if you are sewing by hand) are the running stitch and the overcast stitch

You can stop at this point and settle for just stitching up the garment "as is" OR you can choose to play around with some different ideas. You could cut the sleeves off a long-sleeved shirt and sew them together to make a long skinny pillow.

Tie it in a knot.

The same thing
could be done with the legs of trousers.
You could sew two T-shirts together
to make a large pillow.

You could cut up a skirt
to get a large piece of
fabric to work with.

TRY out your
own ideas now. ◇

OLD
FAITHFUL
❀

Natural DYES

you need
- •YELLOW ONION SKINS
- •AN ENAMELED or STAINLESS STEEL POT
- • WATER
- • ALUM (buy where CANNING SUPPLIES are sold)
- • VINEGAR
- • WHITE 100% WOOL YARN
- • WHITE EGGS
- • LAUNDRY SOAP

First collect your dyestuff.
Onion skins are easy to get. Ask the
person in charge of your supermarket's
produce department if you may clean
out the loose onion skins at the
bottom of the onion bin. Four or five
cups should be about the right amount
for a small batch of dye.

Put the skins into the pot and add enough water to cover them.
Heat it to boiling then lower the heat and simmer uncovered for at least ½ hour.
Get your yarn ready.
It must be 100% wool because synthetic yarns will not take the dye as well as wool.

Make your yarn into a circular skein by wrapping it around the backs of one or two chairs (depending on the amount of yarn you have). When it is all wound, tie the beginning and end together.
Then tie all the strands together in 3 or 4 places with loose figure-eights.

This will keep the yarn from tangling while it floats in the dye.
Wash the yarn in warm, soapy water.
Do <u>not</u> scrub or rub the yarn together as this will cause it to mat and shrink.

37

Squeeze the soapy water through the yarn and rinse several times.
Add ½ teaspoon of alum to the dye.
Stir the dye and let it cool. Strain out the skins from the liquid.
Put the <u>wet</u> yarn into the <u>cooled</u> dye, then slowly heat the dye back to simmering. Simmer for at least ½ hour. Then let the dye and yarn cool a little and rinse in warm water several times. Let it dry and you'll have your own naturally dyed yarn.
You can also dye fabric made of wool, cotton, or cotton blends by using the same method. The shade you get will vary depending on what type of fabric you choose.
Onion skins make beautiful egg dye. Put the eggs, onion skins and cold water into the pan. Add a tablespoon of vinegar. Bring to a simmer and cook for 20 to 30 minutes.

The eggs will become a beautiful reddish brown. Give them a nice sheen by rubbing the shells with a little vegetable oil. For variety, other eggs can be given a mottled brown and gold and white design by first tying the onion skins around the eggs with string or thread. Then follow the same cooking method.

If you have enjoyed doing natural dyeing, you may want to experiment with other natural dyes. Marigolds, goldenrod, Coleus leaves and many other flowers, leaves, bark, roots, berries and lichens make good dyes. See how many you can find and experiment with. Try the same methods of cooking and dyeing with some common plants that grow near where you live. □

MAKING A

BOOK

you need {

- LIGHTWEIGHT CARDBOARD
- PLAIN WHITE PAPER
- PATTERNED or COLORED PAPER
- WHITE GLUE
  or
- RUBBER CEMENT
- WIDE CLOTH TAPE
- LARGE and NEEDLE
- HEAVY THREAD
- RULER
- SCISSORS

First make the pages
for your book.
Take 4 or 5 sheets
of paper and fold
them in half. On the crease, mark
3 dots. Put one dot in the middle of
the crease, the other two dots 1½" to 2"
on either side of it.
Hold the stack of pages
together and poke holes
through all the layers
with the needle at the
dots you have marked.
Thread the needle and
Sew the pages together as illustrated.
Tie the loose ends around
the long stitch thread.
For the cover of your book,
you will need two pieces
of cardboard.
Cut the pieces ½"
larger than your
folded pages on
three sides.

START

KEEP
THESE
EDGES
EVEN

PAGES

½"

cardboard

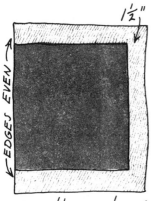

1½"

EDGES EVEN

Cut two pieces of colored paper for the outer cover of the book. Make the paper 1½" larger than the cardboard on <u>three</u> sides. Glue the cover paper to the

cardboard with one edge of the cardboard even with one edge of the paper. Turn in two corners of the cover paper and glue them down. Fold and glue the remaining cover paper to the cardboard.

Measure and cut a piece of wide cloth tape, 2" longer than the book covers.

TURN DOWN →

← ¼

Place the covers on the sticky side of the tape, leaving ¼" between them. One inch of tape will extend beyond the covers, top and bottom. Turn down this extra tape over the edges of the covers.

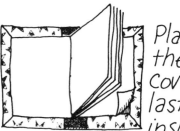 Place the sewn pages into the space between the covers. Glue the first and last pages down to the insides of the book covers.
Clean away any glue that may have squeezed out. Close the book and put a weight on it for a while until the glue dries. For an extra decorative touch, cut two pieces of paper in a contrasting color or pattern and glue  them over the white paper inside the covers. Your book is now ready to give as a gift, write a diary in, use as a photo album, whatever you wish. Try making another book. Experiment with cover materials — How about cloth or contact paper? Make it in a different shape. Use colored papers for pages. Give it your special touch.□

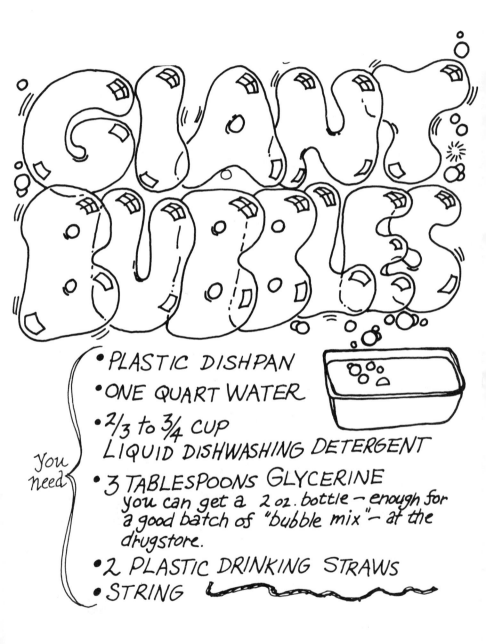

GIANT BUBBLES

you need

- PLASTIC DISHPAN
- ONE QUART WATER
- 2/3 to 3/4 CUP LIQUID DISHWASHING DETERGENT
- 3 TABLESPOONS GLYCERINE
  you can get a 2 oz. bottle — enough for a good batch of "bubble mix" — at the drugstore.
- 2 PLASTIC DRINKING STRAWS
- STRING

Mix the water, detergent and glycerine in the dishpan—gently so as not to make a lot of suds. Measure a piece of string twice as long as both the straws laid end-to-end.

Thread the string through the straws and knot the ends. You should get something resembling a square. Dip the "square" into the bubble mix in the dishpan. Pull up Quickly with the square. The bubble will probably break before it floats free. Keep trying and soon you will be able to pull out a long bubble which will break loose and float slowly away.

There are lots of other things which can be used for blowing bubbles. The plastic rings which hold together six soda cans make good blowers. Dip them all into the bubble mix and wave madly through the air to get multiple bubbles.

Use a wire coat hanger bent into a circle. Try bending another hanger into a "free-form" shape — can you still make bubbles with it?

Try a tin can with both ends cut off.

Creating giant bubbles is a super thing to do with lots of people outdoors on a beautiful day. □

Monoprints

Monoprints

you need

- A PIECE OF WINDOW GLASS or PLEXIGLAS — about 8" x 10"
- MASKING TAPE (if using glass)
- SEVERAL COLORS OF POSTER PAINT
- SMALL SPONGES — cut them from an old kitchen sponge
- PAPER TO PRINT ON

If you are using a piece of glass, first bind the edges with masking tape for safety.

Moisten the sponges, one for each color you want to use. Dip the sponges into the paint and work directly on the glass.

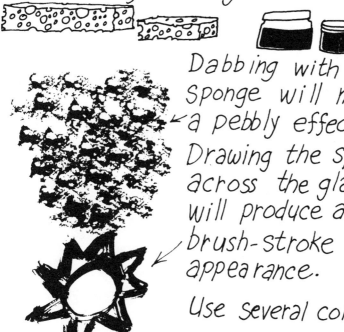

Dabbing with the sponge will make a pebbly effect.

Drawing the sponge across the glass will produce a brush-stroke appearance.

Use several colors.

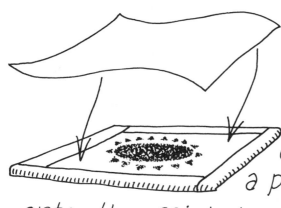

When the paint on the glass satisfies you, carefully lay a piece of paper onto the painted surface. Smooth gently to make sure the paper picks up the design.

You can now pull up your first monoprint. Monoprint means one-of-a-kind print.

A series of prints will be similar but never exactly alike.

Now, if there seems to be excess paint on the glass, try making another print without adding any more paint. Then, for the next print add more paint.

For a complete change of color, wipe all the accumulated paint from the glass with a damp sponge.

Your monoprints could be used for greeting cards, book covers, gift wraps or tags. You can come up with some other uses of your own. Why not hang them on the wall and enjoy them? □

Coiled BASKETS

you need
- CLOTHESLINE ROPE OR THICK CORD
- YARN
- BLUNT YARN NEEDLE

Coiled baskets have been made over the years by people in many parts of the world. Some of the finest coiled baskets are made by Native Americans.
These baskets are usually

made from natural materials such
as vines, grasses or other fibers.
For our learning, rope and yarn
are more convenient.
The thicker the rope, the faster
your basket will grow.

One way to begin
a basket is to tie a knot in one
end of the rope.

Thread your needle with a length
of yarn (3 feet is a good length to work
with). Pull the yarn through the
middle of the knot, leaving a
few inches free.

Go in and out of this same space
several times in order to wrap
the rope with yarn.

Catch in the short end of the rope and work it in with the rest of the knot.

Begin to coil the rope around the knot. First wrap the yarn several times around the new section of rope.

Now make a figure eight of yarn → around both the knot and the piece of wrapped rope.

ROPE

ROPE

Continue to wrap rope several times and then fasten it with "figure eight" loops.

Then make the coil as large as you want the basket bottom to be.

Build sides by fastening new parts of the coil above the last layer.
When you need to start a new strand of yarn, just leave the ends of the old and the new yarns hang loose. These ends can be woven in later.
When the basket is as deep as you want it, cut the end of the rope on the diagonal.

Wrap and fasten securely, letting this diagonal end taper to finish the edge.

MESH
weaving and stitchery

you need
- MESH BAGS— used to package potatoes, onions and other things
- YARN
- A YARN NEEDLE (Bluntpoint)
- SCISSORS

This project will require lots of experimentation on your part because the mesh bags you discover may not be <u>exactly</u> like those I found.

Some common bags _may_ look like these:

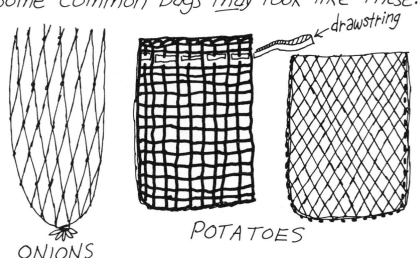

drawstring

ONIONS
(stretchy diamond mesh)

POTATOES

You can weave on these in their own bag form or you can cut them down one side and across the bottom to make a flat piece. It seems to be easier to work with the stretchy "onion" bags if you cut off the gathered part at the bottom. The result is an open-ended tube which can be woven upon and then stitched straight across one end to recreate a bag form.

Also, to begin working on one of
these "onion" tubes it may
help to stretch it around
an oatmeal box.

One way to convert
vegetable containers into
tote bags or wall hangings is to fill in
the mesh with plain over-and-under
weaving. Here are some stitches
which are useful in covering your
mesh material.

These stitches are
like those used in
needlepoint.
You must be
ready to adapt
these as you go;

because the mesh you are working on is more flexible and irregular than needlepoint canvas.

But because these mesh things are so inexpensive you can feel free to really experiment and invent.

Try weaving and stitching very loosely or tightly to see what effects you can get.

Try knotting pieces of yarn onto the mesh to make a fringe.

Your end result can be very free-flowing or it can look very much like needlepoint. Using mesh packaging as a base for stitching and weaving can go in many directions. □

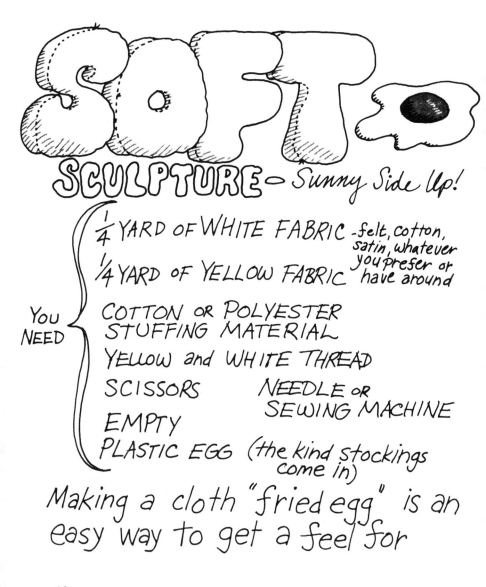

SOFT

SCULPTURE — Sunny Side Up!

You NEED
- 1/4 YARD OF WHITE FABRIC - felt, cotton, satin, whatever you prefer or have around
- 1/4 YARD OF YELLOW FABRIC
- COTTON OR POLYESTER STUFFING MATERIAL
- YELLOW and WHITE THREAD
- SCISSORS
- NEEDLE OR SEWING MACHINE
- EMPTY PLASTIC EGG (the kind stockings come in)

Making a cloth "fried egg" is an easy way to get a feel for

making soft sculpture. If you enjoy this project you will probably think of other objects to make from cloth. Start by cutting two circles about 3" in diameter from the yellow fabric. Sew the two circles together about ¼" from the edge. Leave an opening of about 1½". Turn the sewn circles inside out. Stuff the cloth "yolk" with some of the filler material until it looks as thick as a real fried egg's yolk. Turn in the open part of the seam and sew it shut.

Now, from the white cloth cut two matching free-form pieces measuring from five to six inches wide.

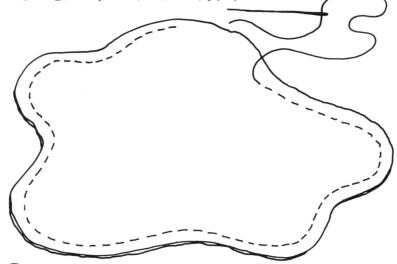

Sew these pieces together about ¼" from the edge, leaving an opening of 1½ to 2 inches. Turn the "white" of the egg inside out and stuff it evenly. Turn under and sew up the open seam.

Place the stuffed yolk on the stuffed white in a place that looks right to you. Sew it in place with little stitches. Now roll or fold up the fried egg and stuff it into the empty plastic stocking egg and you have a funny gift for a friend.□

MOVIE MACHINES

☆ Produce
☆ Your Own
☆ Epics... ☆

YOU NEED

3"x5" CARDS
A SPRING CLIP } KINEOGRAPH ☆

POSTER BOARD - white on one side, black on the other
SCISSORS • THUMBTACK
PENCIL • MIRROR } PHENAKISTOSCOPE ☆

EMPTY OATMEAL OR
ICE CREAM CARTON OR
ANY ROUND BOX
EMPTY SPOOL • DOWEL • GLUE } ZOETROPE ☆

☆ A KINEOGRAPH is a FLIP-CARD MOVIE.

Clip 10 or more 3"x5" cards together with a spring clip. Draw a series of pictures-one on each card (see the last page of the article for animation tips). Then flip the cards rapidly with your thumb—Now you've made a movie.

64

☆A PHENAKISTOSCOPE is a slotted disc which is spun around. It is viewed in a mirror. Cut a circle 6" or 7" in diameter from poster board—black on one side, white on the other (or you can paint one side black).
A saucer or small plate makes a good pattern for your circle.

THUMBTACK HERE

1" x ⅛" SLOTS

7" CIRCLE

Divide the disc into 12 sections and cut 1" x ⅛" slots into the edge. Draw a series of pictures between the slots on the white side. Put a thumbtack in the center of the white side and tack the disc to the pencil. Hold it up to a mirror, spin it and look through the slots at the reflection of the drawings.

MIRROR

☆A ZOETROPE is a cylinder
with slots through which
images are viewed.
Cut down a round
box to a height
of about 4". Divide
the circumference
into 12 equal
sections. Cut 2" x ⅛" slots
into the top edge.
Glue the spool in the
center of the outside
bottom of the box.

STRIP OF
ARTWORK

GLUE
SPOOL TO
CENTER
OF
BOX

dowel

Fit a small dowel into the spool so
you can spin the cylinder around.
Cut paper strips 2" wide and
long enough to fit around the
inside of the box. You can draw
a "movie" on each strip of paper.
Put it in the ZOETROPE MACHINE and
view it through the slots of the
spinning cylinder.

☆To create the effect of MOTION with still pictures, you must draw one image several times with a small change (position, size, shape, color, etc.). Start with simple objects:

a rolling ball...

a winking eye...

a moving figure

or whatever you like...

Objects can grow or shrink...

They can appear, disappear, change colors...

They can also move "toward" you or "away" from you but that will take more planning! □

BANNERS

- FABRIC - LARGER PIECES FOR BACKGROUNDS, SMALL PIECES FOR LETTERS AND DESIGNS
- DOWEL STICKS or CURTAIN RODS
- STRAIGHT PINS AND/OR CHALK
- NEEDLE + THREAD or SEWING MACHINE
- EXTRAS FOR **PIZZAZ** (Beads, Sequins, Fringe, Lace, Rick-Rack, Yarn, Snaps, etc.)

you need

Begin by planning your banner on paper. Keep the designs simple and bold. Decide on colors, lettering and decorations. Make paper patterns of the pieces you'll need to cut out.

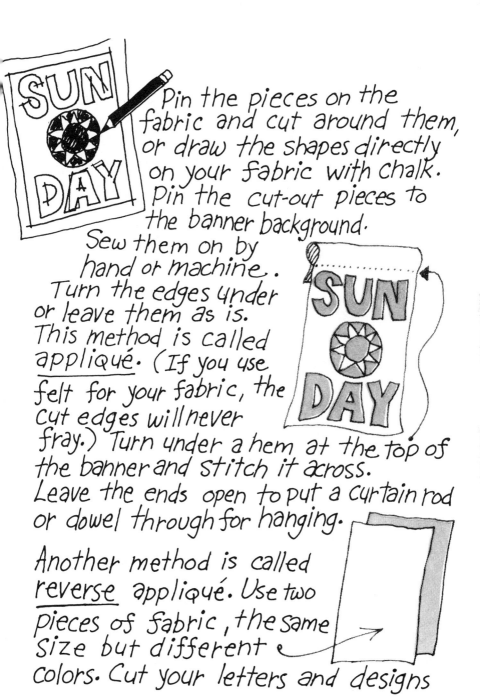

Pin the pieces on the fabric and cut around them, or draw the shapes directly on your fabric with chalk. Pin the cut-out pieces to the banner background.

Sew them on by hand or machine.. Turn the edges under or leave them as is. This method is called appliqué. (If you use felt for your fabric, the cut edges will never fray.) Turn under a hem at the top of the banner and stitch it across. Leave the ends open to put a curtain rod or dowel through for hanging.

Another method is called reverse appliqué. Use two pieces of fabric, the same size but different colors. Cut your letters and designs through the top layer, allowing the color of the bottom layer to show through. Then, turn the cut edges under and sew the top and bottom layers together around the cut edges. Save the cut out pieces for extra decorations on your reverse appliqué banner.

Another way to make your design is called couching. You can "draw" your designs and letters with yarn. Pin the yarn into place on your fabric. Then hold it in place with widely spaced stitches of thread. Use these three techniques to make many kinds of banners:
•A Round banner,— hang fabric strips from a macramé hoop.

- A "Funny Face" banner with different eyes, noses, etc. to snap on.
- A Seasonal banner could have flowers, snowflakes, leaves to attach as seasons change.
- Sew spices into a hidden place to make a banner that smells good.
- Make a tiny banner and mail it to a friend.
- Make banners for special events.
- Say it with banners!

PLASTER

CARVE or CAST

You need
- PLASTER OF PARIS
- VERMICULITE (from a Garden Store)
- MIXING CONTAINER • WATER
- PAPER CUPS, MILK CARTONS, SMALL BOXES
- PLASTIC SANDWICH BAGS
- PARING KNIFE • NAIL
- MODELING CLAY • ALUMINUM FOIL

Plaster of Paris is a very easy and inexpensive medium to use to discover whether you are a budding sculptor.

The basic recipe for making plaster of Paris is to mix 2 parts of plaster powder to 1 part of water. Add the dry powder to the water for the smoothest mixing.

For a _textured_ carving block, mix 2 parts of Vermiculite and 1 part of Plaster of Paris. To these ingredients add just enough water to make a _thick_ smooth mixture.

When you want to do some carving, mix up a batch of one of the above recipes and pour it into a paper milk carton, paper cups, or other small cardboard containers. Allow the plaster to harden and then tear away the paper mold.

plaster mixture

Cottage Cheese

<u>Carve</u> the block of plaster with a paring knife, nail or other sturdy instrument.

<u>Casting</u> in plaster means that you <u>carve</u> in some <u>other</u> medium and then pour plaster into this mold.

Roll out modeling clay into a 1" thick Slab. With a nail make a design in the clay.

• or make impressions in the clay by pressing small objects (a key, a shell, anything interesting) into the surface. You could also make designs and patterns by repeating the shapes.

• or <u>build up</u> a design with clay. When it is cast, carved out areas will be raised; built up areas will be indented.

Put the clay onto a piece of

aluminum foil and fold up the edges to form a container. Pour plaster over the clay design. Tap it a bit to dislodge air bubbles. Let it dry and gently remove the plaster from the clay. Try free-form casting in a plastic sandwich bag. Pour a small batch of plaster into the bag. Mold it by holding the bag until the plaster sets (about 10 minutes). Then set it aside to dry for an hour and peel away the plastic. You can color your sculpture with paint or markers and add a finish with varnish when it is dry. □

HANDMADE SLIDES

- REJECTED SLIDES
- CHLORINE BLEACH
- COTTON SWABS
- FINE-POINT FELT MARKERS
- "STAINED GLASS" PAINT
- CLEAR CONTACT PAPER
- MAGAZINES WITH COLOR PICTURES
- SHEET OF CLEAR PLASTIC
- PURCHASED SLIDE MOUNTS
- WATER
- SMALL BOWL

you need

A good way to start making handmade
slides is to re-use slides which have
turned out too dark or too light.
Begin by making a solution of one
Tablespoon of chlorine bleach mixed with
one Tablespoon of water in a small bowl.
Dip a cotton swab into the solution and
rub it over the dull (emulsion) side of
the slide. Slowly
the color will be
removed by the
bleach. Change

WATER
+
BLEACH

to a new swab often. Soon you will
have a clear slide. Let it dry for a
while. To make a new image, draw or
write on the film with a fine-tip
felt marker. You can get very bright
colors by painting on your slide with
"stained glass" paint, which you can buy
at a craft store. They may also sell
paint which crystallizes as it dries.
This is fun because the final result

is always a surprise.

You can make a design on a completely black slide by scratching on the dull side with a pin or other sharp point; or poke holes through the black slide to make a "dotty" design.

For more experiments you can buy slide mounts at a photography store. There are several types:

•One is open and hinged. The picture is sandwiched between the two windows and sealed with a warm iron.

•Another type has a slot into which you can <u>slide</u> the picture. This type of mount can be used over and over since you can replace the picture.

Some magazine pictures can be made into slides. Take a square of clear contact paper, a bit larger than the window of a slide frame. Peel off the backing and stick the contact paper onto the picture you want. Rub it carefully to make sure it is firmly stuck. Cut out this section of the page + soak it in warm water for about 5 minutes. The magazine's paper should easily peel away leaving just the _ink_ on the sticky contact paper. Let it dry and insert it into a slide mount. Try making "sandwich" slides. Cut pieces of clear plastic (like a photo album page) to fit into your slide mounts. Take two pieces of plastic and sandwich a small bit of something (feather, leaf, lace, string or yarn) between them. Put your "sandwich" into a slide mount. Now put all your handmade slides together and give a show for your friends. ¤

PROCESSED BY You

OFFBEAT PAINTING

YOU NEED

- POSTER PAINT - IN DIFFERENT COLORS
- LOTS OF PAPER
- DRINKING STRAWS
- MARBLES or PING PONG BALLS
- A SHALLOW BOX
- STRING
- SPOON
- SMALL DISHES or PANS

No sketches, no brushes, no erasers are needed, you just need a sense of curiosity for what can be done with color and some offbeat ways to paint.

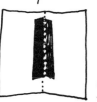 Pick up some poster paint on the end of a drinking straw and drop several colors on a piece of paper. Fold the paper and press it with your hand. Try folding the paper diagonally or off-center.
Add more paint and re-fold it in a different direction than you did the first time.

2 Dip a piece of string in the paint. Drop it on a piece of paper and pull it across to make a snake-like track.

Cover the paper with many colored tracks.

Drop a paint coated string on another piece of paper. Fold the paper over the string and, while holding the paper down, pull the string out from between the layers. Surprise!

Drop several colors of paint onto paper with a drinking straw. Blow on the drops with the straw to push the paint around.

Blow from the side or blow from above to get different effects. Try to get the colors to mix.

4 Now, put a piece of paper in the shallow box. Pour some paint into the small dishes. Drop a marble or a ping pong ball into each color, to coat it with paint. Fish out the ball or marble with the spoon and roll it around on the paper. Allow it to ricochet back and forth off the sides of the box.

Try combining all of these painting methods. You may produce some attractive little abstract paintings that can be matted and hung up to enjoy. □

KITCHEN CHEMISTRY

YOU NEED

- 1 QUART GLASS JAR
- BAKING SODA
- CITRIC ACID (Sour Salt)
- PIECES OF BROKEN BRICK OR CLAY FLOWER POT
- LAUNDRY BLUEING
- HOUSEHOLD AMMONIA
- MOTHBALLS
- SALT
- CORNSTARCH
- WATER
- GLASS OR PLASTIC DISH

With chemicals you probably have in your kitchen you can concoct a batch of mysterious bobbing mothballs, a crystal garden and a bowl of home made "quicksand."
Collect a quart jar, mothballs, baking soda and citric acid (sour salt). Citric

84

acid is used in preparing and preserving food. (If it's not in your super market, you can buy it in the spice section of a delicatessen or gourmet food store.) Fill the jar with water. Add 1½ teaspoons of baking soda - add 2 teaspoons of citric acid. This will cause bubbling and fizzing in the jar for a short time. Drop 4 or 5 mothballs into the jar. They will begin to rise and sink in the water. If this does not happen after a few minutes add tiny amounts of baking soda and citric acid until the mothballs begin to move. Once the proper balance of chemicals is reached this motion will continue for an hour or more.

MOTH BALLS

Strange formations appear when you combine salt, laundry blueing, ammonia and water - and pour it over porous material. Place the brick or flower pot pieces in a glass or plastic dish. Mix 3 tablespoons of laundry blueing (from the "laundry products" section of the supermarket), 3 tablespoons of salt, 3 tablespoons of water and 1½ teaspoons of ammonia. Mix these together thoroughly and pour over the brick or flower pot shards. Within an hour crystals will begin to grow - and will continue to grow for several days. After the crystal growth stops it can be renewed by adding a few drops of ammonia.

Homemade quicksand is super simple to make and fascinating to experiment with. In a bowl, combine 2 parts of cornstarch with one part of water.
A good amount to start with is ½ cup cornstarch mixed with ¼ cup water. This forms a substance which, when handled, can seem like a solid one moment and a liquid the next.

Try shaping some "quicksand" into a ball. Then hold the ball in your hand. What happens?

Some rainy day, turn the kitchen into a laboratory and try these experiments. □

moth

KNITTING

Machine

YOU NEED

- **2** PIECES OF WOOD: 15" × ¾" × ¾"
- **2** PIECES OF WOOD: 5" × 1½" × 1"
- SANDPAPER   • HAMMER   • RULER
- **40** 1" BRADS
- **4** 1¼" NAILS or SCREWS
- **2** THUMB TACKS   • YARN
- KNITTING NEEDLE or BLUNT YARN NEEDLE
- MEDIUM-SIZED CROCHET HOOK

Sand all the rough edges off the wood pieces.

Make a mark 1½" from each end of the 15" pieces of wood.

Make marks ⅝" apart along the

wood, between the first two marks.

$1\frac{1}{2}$" ｜｜｜｜｜｜｜$\frac{5}{8}$"｜｜｜｜｜｜｜｜｜｜｜ $1\frac{1}{2}$"

Pound a brad into each mark, leaving
$\frac{1}{2}$" to $\frac{3}{4}$" of each brad standing
above the surface.
Nail or screw the thin wood pieces
on top of the 2 short flat pieces.
Leave $\frac{1}{4}$" space between the pieces
with the
brads. thumb
tack →

$\frac{1}{4}$"
SPACE

thumb
tack

Now you are ready to knit long beautiful
scarves (or pieces which can be sewn
together to make afghans).

←Beginning Knot

Tie one end of the yarn to an
end peg. Wind the yarn around
each peg, as shown, encircling the
pegs. Next, take the yarn back to
the beginning point by just going

back and forth, _not_ encircling
each peg.

WRAP YARN
AROUND TACK
TO HOLD IT

You should now have _two_
strands of yarn on each peg. With
the blunt yarn needle or knitting needle,
lift the lower loop of yarn up over the
top strand of yarn _and_ _over_ the top
of the peg, leaving what was the
top loop alone on the peg. Repeat this
with each peg.
Rewind the
yarn back and forth (like your second
layer) to the other end of the loom
and repeat the knitting process.
As your work accumulates, the
knitted yarn will work itself
down between the pieces of
wood.

To finish off your work - use the crochet hook. Begin at the side of the loom which does not have the ball of yarn attached to it. With the crochet hook, lift the loop off the first peg. Then lift off the loop of the peg opposite and pull it through the first loop. Repeat this process, working always from one peg to the one opposite it. When you have worked all the loops off and have just one remaining on your crochet hook, cut the yarn from the ball and pull that cut end all the way through the last loop. Pull it snug, and there's your scarf! You may have recognized the knitting you've just done as "spool knitting". You can do knitting in wider or narrower widths by changing the dimensions of the loom. ▢

APPLIQUÉ and
REVERSE → APPLIQUÉ

you need
- FABRIC IN A VARIETY OF COLORS
- SCISSORS • NEEDLES and PINS
- THREAD
- AN OLD SHIRT, JACKET OR JEANS

Appliqué means to apply pieces of fabric to another piece of fabric. When you patch your jeans you are doing appliqué.

Reverse appliqué means you cut through several layers of fabric and stitch them to create a design.

Try appliqué and reverse appliqué by decorating old clothing. Find a garment to personalize. Thrift shops are full of surprising and inexpensive items.

Learn appliqué first. Decide where you would like to decorate your shirt or jeans. If you have a lined jacket you could appliqué on the lining for a unique touch.
Cut simple shapes from colored fabric. Arrange them on the garment to form a design.
Turn under ¼" at edge of fabric shape and pin. Then with small stitches, sew around all the edges. Repeat with the other appliqué pieces.

turn under ¼" of fabric

Make a "practice piece" of **reverse appliqué** before you work on a piece of clothing.

Choose 3 colors from your fabric pieces – all the <u>same size</u>.

With LONG stitches, baste the pieces together around the edges.

Draw a large, simple shape on the top layer of fabric.

Cut this shape carefully out of the TOP LAYER **only.** Turn under and pin the cut edges to the second layer with small stitches as you did on your appliquéd patch.

Now draw another shape on the <u>second</u> layer of cloth and cut through **just** that layer.

Turn under the cut edges and sew, just as before.

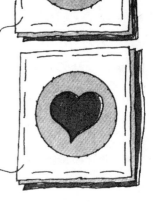

cut

stitch edges

cut

With the basted edges turned under this completed piece can be used as an appliqué on the clothing you are decorating. It could be sewn on a shirt pocket or a tote bag.

Reverse appliqué can be done **directly** on a garment by using the fabric of the shirt, jacket or whatever you have as the TOP LAYER of the basted set of fabrics.

Reverse appliqué can be made MUCH more intricate.

Try using more layers of color and cutting smaller and more complicated shapes. □